THE PRESENTATION

A Story About Communicating Successfully

With Very Few Slides

THE PRESENTATION

A Story About Communicating Successfully

With Very Few Slides

ANDREW V. ABELA, PH.D.

THE PRESENTATION:
A Story About Communicating Successfully With Very Few Slides

ISBN 10: 1453764135
ISBN 13: 9781453764138

For additional copies of this book,
visit www.ExtremePresentation.com

The presentation: a story about communicating
successfully with very few slides / Andrew V. Abela

1. Business presentations. 2. Business communication. I. Title

Design by Marja Walker

Table of Contents

Chapter One

A Serious Problem

BARBARA LOOKED RIGHT AT HIM. The concern in her voice was clear.

"You know we have our backs to the wall on this one, David. I had to pull a few strings to get you on the Board's agenda."

David, General Manager of the Specialized Materials Division (SMD) of Asprit Industries, had only recently begun reporting to Barbara, Group Vice President, but his hard work and straightforward honesty had already made him one of her favorites.

"I know that, and I appreciate it. It's not just for me; if we can't get the Board to give us the investment we need, my whole team will be out on the street, job hunting. I *have* to make this work."

Barbara leaned forward. "What can I do to help you get your presentation ready for the Board meeting?"

"Well, I have about 75 slides worth of material. I think my case is pretty solid, but I know I need to cut it way down—I just want to make sure I don't leave anything important out."

"75 slides…" Barbara looked concerned. "You know they'll never sit through that. You won't be through slide five before they're questioning your assumptions, your logic…. But then— I'm not the best resource when it comes to presentations…."

David chuckled. They both knew Barbara was notorious across the entire firm for her monstrous 'Death by PowerPoint' presentation decks.

David sat up. "There is actually one thing you can do. I saw an interesting speaker the other day, at the Association Conference. He had a different take on presentations, which I think might help with our Board. He's a retired professor, and he has an office here in town. Would you be okay with me working with him? It might cost a bit, but I think I really have to try something provocative to get the Board's attention. As you said—it was a struggle just to get on the agenda."

"If you think it will help, sure. Why don't you go and work with this guy and then I'll join you for a dry run when you're ready?"

"Thank you. I will." He nodded, gathered up his papers, and left her office.

Chapter Two

A Glimmer of Hope

PROFESSOR EDWARDS DID NOT LOOK LIKE A PROFESSOR. In his deep blue suit, white shirt and red tie, clean-shaven with short, grey hair, he looked more like a seasoned executive.

"So what do you have so far?" he asked.

"75 slides. Yes, I know—too many slides, and too many of them are just lists of bullets or tables of data. But it's all important stuff. I have some ideas for how to improve it, though. I've been reading some books on presentation and looking at some blogs. I think what I need to do is replace these slides with ones that are way more visual—lots of good images and photographs, that will help me get my points across, with very little text."

Figure 1: A Selection of David's Slides

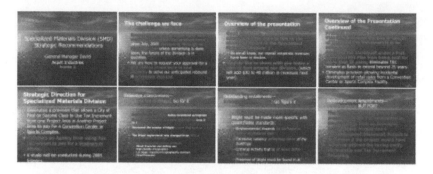

The Professor nodded. "Yes, that sounds like it would be a big improvement."

"Except...I'm not sure how to get all of the specifics across. I have a lot of analyses: financial, competitive, customer data—important stuff like that. How do I communicate those in a slideshow full of images?"

Professor Edwards looked carefully at David; the grey marks under David's eyes were evidence of many late nights preparing this material, and the professor wanted to be sympathetic.

"Tell me a bit about the context of this presentation. It sounds like you're planning a speech at a sales meeting or something. Big crowd, I suppose—five hundred or a thousand, or more?"

David looked surprised. "Oh no, nothing like that. It's just half a dozen board members. I shouldn't say 'just'—they're six people who get to decide whether my entire staff and I will still have jobs two months from now. I *have to* convince them to invest in our division."

"Oh, I see. Well then, in that case, I think you should forget about the images."

"What do you mean? Everything I've read so far says the best way to design a presentation is with images and few words on each slide!" David mentally began to question this fellow's knowledge of presentation design. Had this guy never even heard of *Slide:ology*, or *Presentation Zen*?

The professor smiled.

"Yes," he said. "That approach *is* the best way to design a presentation—*if* what you're trying to do is inform, entertain, or motivate a large audience. We call that style of presentation design 'Ballroom style'—because it's the kind of presentation you would give in a hotel ballroom at a sales convention, or an industry gathering. But it's not the *only* effective style of presentation design. It sounds to me that what you are trying to do is convince a *small* number of people to make a *specific decision* and to take a *particular action*—to accept your proposal and invest a certain amount of money in your division. Am I right?"

"Yes...." David wasn't sure why this mattered.

"Well, that kind of task calls for a completely different style of presentation. You need a 'Conference room style' presentation, the kind of presentation you give in a conference room or boardroom, when you're trying to *persuade*: your colleagues, your clients or prospects, or—in your case—your board members; when you're trying *to persuade people to do something*. The two styles are completely different."

"I remember—you mentioned something about this at the conference last week. I didn't totally understand it then, and I don't think I do now; why do I need a different style of presentation when I'm trying to persuade a small group of people to do something specific?"

"You just said it yourself, David: it's the specifics, the details. If you're going to make a sale, any kind of sale—whether you're selling a product, a proposal, or an idea—you're going to have to provide your audience with all of the particulars they need: investment levels, timing, resources, your competitive and financial analyses, and so on. No one is going to buy what you're selling if you don't give them all of the specifics they need to make their decision. Ballroom style presentations, pictures with minimal text, just can't convey enough detail to get the specifics across. That's why, in this case, you need a Conference Room style presentation."

"But if what you're saying is true, then how come so few people know about this style?"

"Actually, in certain areas it's more popular than you think. Gene Zelazny has been teaching something like this approach, which he calls 'lap visuals,' at McKinsey & Company—and in his books *Say It With Charts* and *Say It With Presentations*—for several decades now. If you look at good consultants' presentations, many of them take a Conference room style approach. And the visual display guru, Edward Tufte, has long argued in favor of paper-based communication rather than projected slides.

"Mostly, though, I think it's just a matter of time. Remember, it was only very recently that both *Slide:ology* and *Presentation Zen* were published. Before that, we had twenty-one years of a steadily growing 'Death by PowerPoint' pandemic. I think most people are so relieved to see something more visually attractive instead that they haven't yet reached the point where they've questioned whether Ballroom style presentations are really appropriate for sales- or persuasion-oriented presentations. But I think they'll catch on soon. The absence of details, of specifics, in Ballroom style presentations, makes them the wrong approach if you want to persuade people to take action."

"Ok. So tell me more about this Conference room style, and why I should trust it."

"Not yet." The professor leaned forward. "First I need to ask you a few more questions. I follow something called the Extreme Presentation™ method for presentation design. It's for creating presentations in situations like yours: when you're facing a very tough situation and you absolutely need to persuade your audience to do or to agree to a specific thing."

The professor reached for a thick notepad and pen. "Okay, first question: What is the objective of your presentation?"

Chapter Three

The Objective

DAVID HANDED HIM A SLIDE. "Here—this is my objectives slide." Among some other details, the slide contained these three bullets:

- Review market demand
- Summarize competitor analysis
- Outline proposal and investment requirements

"David, these are not objectives."

"What do you mean?"

The professor held up the slide. "These are not objectives; they are your *agenda*. These are the things *you* propose to do in the meeting. Objectives are not what *you* want to do, but what you want your *audience* to do. Think of it in terms of how you want your presentation to change your audience members minds and actions."

He drew a two-by-two matrix on his notepad, and said,

"We call this the 'From-To, Think-Do matrix.' This is where we describe exactly how you want your audiences' 'thinking' and 'doing' to change *from* before your presentation *to* after it. Let's fill it out. In the top left corner, let's fill in what they're thinking before your presentation. What are they thinking right now?"

David paused and rubbed his chin. "I would say they're thinking there is no future for my division."

"Okay, let's write that in there. The top right corner is what you want them to be thinking *after* your presentation."

"That's easy—I want them to think my plan is a good one, and they should give us the investment we're asking for."

"Good... And now the bottom left. What are they doing—or not doing—right now?"

David winced. "Well, they're not giving us any further funding and they're planning to shut us down."

"And after your presentation—what then?"

Figure 2: The From-To Think-Do Matrix

	FROM	TO
THINK	No future for the division	Good plan, we should invest in it
DO	No further funding; planning to shut down	Provide funding

"Hopefully… They will give us the funding we need."

"Excellent!" Edwards leaned forward and tapped the notepad with his forefinger. "Do you see why we need this? This matrix will now be our guide through the rest of your presentation—any part of your presentation that moves you from the left side of the matrix to the right belongs in your presentation, anything that does not is out! Clear?"

David thought if the situation weren't so desperate, he'd find it amusing to see the older man getting so excited about this two-by-two matrix. But he saw how this could help him focus his presentation a bit more.

"Clear," he said.

"Next question then: why is your audience going to listen to you—why should they say 'yes' to your proposal?"

Chapter Four

The Audience Problem
and Your Solution

"WELL," SAID DAVID, "Barbara, my boss, has already done the hard work to convince them to put me on the agenda for their meeting, so I guess they're going to listen to what I have to say…"

"You don't sound very convinced."

David's head fell, just slightly. A brief wince shot across his usually cheerful face. "That's because the few times I've presented to them before, or seen anyone else present to them, well, they hardly give you time to get started, and then they're grilling you with questions, challenging anything you say. It's really hard to get them to listen!"

Edwards smiled. "That's why you need to make it very clear to them *why* they should be listening… up front. The way to do that is to make it clear that you are going to solve an important problem for them in this presentation. What problem do they have that your presentation will help them solve, David?"

David thought for a moment, and then said,

"Well, they're going to shut down our division."

"And whose problem is that, David?"

"I suppose it's more my problem than theirs. But it is a problem for them too, though."

Edwards drew closer. "Tell me more about that. In what way is it a problem for them?"

"The company's been struggling to meet its profit goals, so losing our contribution, as slim as it is, won't help. And it's going to look bad in the community, because there'll be quite a few lay-offs."

"And if they accept your plan, David, and you're successful, what will happen to your division's profits, and the jobs?"

"Profits will increase and we'll keep all the jobs, and possibly even be hiring, if our analysis is right. Many of our competitors are getting out of this business right now, but my team's analysis shows over the next 12 months we should see a moderate strengthening of demand, which should bring more robustness to pricing."

"Good, good!" The professor smiled. "So the problem they have is they're not meeting their profit goals, and the solution you're offering is *increased* profit. That's pretty good! Do you think they'll pay attention to you if you begin your presentation by saying that?"

"I guess so... For a few minutes, I suppose."

"Good enough for now. Next question: this is a bold statement, that you're going to turn around a struggling division in the midst of a recession. How are you going to back that up—what's your evidence for this?"

Chapter Five

The Evidence

"IT'S ALL HERE," SAID DAVID, "IN MY 75 SLIDES."

"You'll excuse me if I don't read it all myself," replied the professor, with a smile. "Give me the highlights—what are the key analyses, or main points that support your claim that you can turn this division around."

David began flipping through his slide deck again.

"Let's see. I've got my market analysis, and the customer research that goes with it; there's the competitor analysis; the details of how we would spend the investment; and the pro forma financial statements for the division, showing before and after the implementation of the proposal."

"Good. That sounds pretty comprehensive." Professor Edwards seemed content.

"Do you want to go though these?"

"No, not right now. I think I have enough of an idea at this point. We've covered your objectives, the problem and solution, and you've got your evidence. The main question now is how do we turn all of this into a compelling story that your board members will want to listen to, from start to finish. You've got to tell the right story."

Chapter Six

Anecdotes

"A STORY? LIKE 'ONCE UPON A TIME…'"

"Yes. Storytelling is critical for effective communication."

David wasn't naturally inclined to be a cynic. And he had heard about the importance of storytelling. He just couldn't see it working in his situation.

"Maybe, for the people *you* work with," he said. "You haven't met *my* board members—most of them are former engineers; tough, numbers-focused people. I'm going to feel like a fool if I walk in there and try to tell them a story." David's enthusiasm for this approach, which had started to build, deflated.

"David, there is extensive research showing that stories are a very powerful form of communication—even in a serious business environment. It goes even deeper than that, though. Some philosophers now believe *the very way we make sense of our lives*, the way we understand its meaning, is through the form of a story, a narrative."

David looked unconvinced. The professor continued:

"Let me put it this way, David: whether or not you or your board members realize it, they're going to make sense of the information you give them by turning it into a story in their own heads."

"Are you serious?"

"Yes, there is good research evidence to support this, David. I promise you—I'm not in the habit of making stuff up. Maybe the word 'story' is what's putting you off?"

"Well, when you say 'story' I think of *Little House on the Prairie*, or *The Hobbit*, stuff like that."

"Those are great... they bring back happy memories of reading to my own children." Edwards grinned. "But we're trying to do something different here. Let's start small—before we work on your entire presentation, let's try to find one or two stories we can use *within* your presentation to drive home your more important points. What is one of the more important points you want to make in this presentation, David?"

"Well—the most controversial one is that we expect demand to rebound over the next 12 months."

"And what proof do you have for that?"

David felt like he was back in his MBA classroom, being quizzed by his professor. But he had his facts ready.

"We have a survey of our major customers, asking them to estimate their requirements quarter by quarter, and it shows, clearly, a rebound in demand is starting to happen," he said, with some satisfaction.

"And—realistically—what do you think the board members will say when you present that to them? Be honest."

David paused, exhaled, and then said,

"They probably... will challenge the data. I've seen them do that before. In fact, when I showed this to Barbara, my boss, the first time, *she* didn't believe it either."

"But she believes it now?" asked Edwards.

"Yes, she does. Otherwise she wouldn't have arranged to get me into the board meeting."

"And how did you convince her?"

"Well, we talked about it for a while. I took her through the methodology, our survey approach—we're very rigorous—but what really seemed to convince her was when I told her what Arjun told us..."

"Who's Arjun?" interrupted the professor, "and what did he say?"

"Arjun is the purchasing manager at one of our biggest customers. He was our first customer interview, and he told us an interesting story. Apparently, they've been having trouble sourcing one of their key raw materials, Gallium Arsenide, which is a critical component in cell phone manufacture. The demand for cell phones and particularly smart phones has strained supply for the material."

"So now they'll be buying that ingredient from you?"

"No, it's not part of our product line. But in certain applications they will be replacing it with another ingredient..."

"And you sell that one?"

"Nope—but that one only works in conjunction with an-other ingredient, Phenomagnol, which we recently developed. I think our other customers are also aware of this, which is why the survey has them forecasting an increase in demand."

"David, do you see what you just did here?" Professor Ed-wards was smiling again.

"No, I don't..."

"You did two very powerful things, right out of the theory of persuasion. First, instead of just telling Barbara only *that* the survey data indicates an increase in demand, you told her *why*—why the demand is going up: what is *causing* that increase. There is good research indicating that *causal* information is more con-vincing than mere facts: if you explain *why* something is happen-ing, what is causing it, people are more likely to believe you."

"I see."

"And the second thing: you told her a *story*. You told her a story one of your customers told you. You showed her the facts, and she wasn't convinced; you told her a story, and she was. How many customers completed your survey?"

"Eighty-four."

"So with a sample size of eighty-four, your survey wasn't convincing, but with a sample of only one, your story, was. How do you explain that?"

"No idea..." answered David, and then, pausing, suggested, "... storytelling works?"

"Exactly!"

David's brow bunched up. "So are you saying we should throw out our data, and just tell stories?" He thought he knew the answer to this question, but he had to ask.

"Of course not. You absolutely must include your data. But the data alone are not enough. You need to drive your conclusions home by providing interesting anecdotal information—exactly like you did with Barbara."

The professor angled his head as he looked at David. "Are you a little more open to the idea of stories at this point?" he asked.

"A little," said David, grinning.

"Good enough for me. Because the big question we have to face now is, how to turn your *entire presentation* into a story.

Chapter Seven

Sequencing Presentation Content into the Form of a Story

"SOUNDS LIKE A CHALLENGE," SAID DAVID.

"It is, somewhat. Probably the most challenging step in the entire design of your presentation. If we do it right, you'll grab your audience at the beginning and won't let them go until the end. Also, it will be very clear 'what's in and what's out' of your presentation, because anything that fits with your storyline will be in your presentation, and anything that doesn't—you can leave out. You'll be able to cut down your number of slides significantly this way"

"That would be nice. So how do we do it?"

"What you need to know first is that the way all stories proceed is by creating and then resolving tension. That's how they keep you interested."

Edwards reached behind him and pulled a book off a shelf. *"The Prisoner of Zenda*, by Anthony Hope Hawkins," he announced, holding the book up. "Have you read it?"

David admitted that he'd never heard of it.

"A classic adventure story. If you read through it, you'll see how the hero, Rudolph Rassendyl, goes from one tense moment to the next.

"He goes on a journey to the central European kingdom of Ruritania, where he bumps into King Rudolph, who is to be crowned the very next day. The two men are distant cousins, and the king's aides are astonished at how alike they look. They dine together, and the king gets very badly drunk. The next morning, his aides are unable to wake him up. This is more than just a hangover—they suspect the king's evil half-brother Prince Michael has slipped something into his wine. This is bad news, because they know if the king doesn't show up for his coronation, then Michael will seize the throne of Ruritania for himself.

"Do you see how the tension is set up here—the king is about to lose his crown! Then it's resolved: Rudolph is convinced to go to the capital, impersonating the king, get himself crowned and then sneak out of the country once the real king is recovered and smuggled back into the palace.

"Then another tension arises: Rudolph the would-be king-impersonator has to ride through the inner city, which is full of Michael's supporters, and so he might be exposed. Then he pulls this off, and gets crowned, and then leaves the city safely, so *that* tension is resolved. Then, the next tension: the hung-over real king has disappeared, and the person they left looking after him has been murdered..."

"Then what?"

The professor smiled. "See, it draws you in, this tension and resolution thing, doesn't it? I'll lend you the book if you like and you can read it yourself... once your presentation is done."

David thought to himself, if the presentation didn't work out, he might have a lot more time for reading than he would want.

Edwards went on. "My point is, this creating and resolving tension keeps your interest throughout the book, right until the end. We need to do the same thing with our presentations. We're going to grab and keep your audience's attention by creating and resolving tensions, which we'll call "Complications" and "Resolutions.""

"Our presentation will begin with a Situation, a very brief 'why we are here,' which will only occur once, at the very start of the presentation. Then we'll show them a Complication, which will create tension, and this will be the business problem of theirs that you came up with—revenues are declining—and then the Resolution, which takes away the tension. That's your proposal. After that, we'll follow up with an Example, which will add more specifics, more details to the resolution. We call it the S.Co.R.E sequence: Situation, Complication, Resolution, Example.

"Once you've gone through the S.Co.R.E. the first time, you keep repeating it—minus the Situation, because you only need to state the situation once, at the beginning of the presentation. So it's just the Complication, Resolution, Example—you keep repeating this."

"So we're just repeating the Co.R.E.?"

"Exactly. We're going to use these colored cards." Professor Edwards removed a stack of colored index cards from his desk drawer, and drew out a yellow one.

Situation

"We're going to write the word 'Situation' at the top left of this one. And so the situation for your presentation is…"

"That they need to invest in our division," David interjected.

"Not so fast. The Situation must be completely non-controversial. Remember how you said, within minutes, the board members are interrupting and asking questions? Well, we don't want to encourage that, do we, by starting off with something controversial?"

"True."

"So what's the completely non-controversial situation you're in?"

David paused for a moment, staring at what looked like a reproduction of a large, old map on the wall. It had an orange band across it, which seemed to get thinner as it moved to the right—and then a black band below that, getting still thinner from right to left. It looked familiar, but he couldn't remember where he had seen something like it before. "We're going to talk about the future of our division, I suppose," he said.

"That works." Professor Edwards wrote the sentence on the yellow card, in neat script. "We take care to write only on the top half of the card, because we'll need the bottom half for something else, later."

Complication

He put the yellow card down on his desk. "Okay, now we take a red card, and write the word 'Complication' in the top left corner. This one is easy; the first complication is the business problem they have…"

"…the company's revenues are declining." David felt like this was starting to make some sense to him.

Resolution

"Good. And now we grab a green card, call it 'Resolution,' and fill in the solution to the business problem they have. Which is what?"

"Um, I suppose something like 'if we can turn my division around, then we can provide some incremental revenues.'"

Professor Edwards looked skeptical. "David—that doesn't give off much confidence, does it?"

"OK, how about: we have a plan to turn around our division, which will add $25 million in gross profit next year."

"Now you're getting there! And I like the specificity—you're giving them a real number."

Example

The professor continued: "There's one more piece we need, so that we've gone through the S.Co.R.E. method the first time, and that's the Example. We need an example—some illustrative detail—of your Resolution."

"Not sure what you mean," David replied.

"The Example plays a couple of important roles in the storyline. First, if you keep hitting your audience with Complication/Resolution/Complication/Resolution and so on, they're probably going to get quite irritated, quickly. So the Example gives them a bit of a break, a few moments to absorb the Resolution... before you hit them with the next Complication.

"The other reason you need an Example there is that the working world is full of generalities, of abstractions and buzzwords. And so we use the Example to bring us down to details, to specific facts, to particular cases, like that of Arjun. This goes on a blue card. Is there a specific detail, or story, or something you can tell here that will give your board members a flavor of the reality you are going to be sharing with them?"

David glanced at the old map again. It had what looked like some kind of a line graph at the bottom. A thought came to him: "Could I tell them about the new $1.2 million order LineCorp just gave us? Kind of like the first installment on our new turn-around plan?"

"Very good, yes—let's put that down on a blue card. Is the order confirmation in a format that you could print or save to a digital image?"

"I think so—why?"

"Even better than telling an anecdote, is showing one: *show* them a copy of the order confirmation. David, do you see how you are going to grab their attention *immediately* here? You'll say to them: 'I'm here to talk about the future of our division' (That's the Situation). Then: 'As we all know, we're not meeting our corporate profit goals' (the Complication). 'I would like to share with you today a plan to turn around our division, that will add $25 million in gross profit next year' (the Resolution). 'And here's an example of what I think we can achieve—this is an order we just received from LineCorp, for $1.2 million' (that's the Example)."

David nodded his head a couple of times. He liked where this was going. It was concrete enough to get the attention of the board members. "This is good. It's a good setup. So now I tell them my plan?"

Next Complication

"Yes—yes, that is exactly *what* you are going to do now. But the important question is *how* you are going do it. The answer to that is to continue to repeat the Co.R.E.; we leave the "S" behind because we only use the Situation once, at the very beginning. After that we just keep repeating the Complication/Resolution/Example—the Co.R.E.

"So let's try that. Here's the absolutely essential thing: the Complication at the beginning of each Co.R.E. has to be *the most likely objection your audience would raise if you paused your presentation at that point*. So—if you were to pause your presentation just after telling them your situation, and your plan to generate $25 million, and the order from LineCorp, what would their most likely objection be at that point?"

"That's easy—they would say, 'Wait a minute, we know you're in a declining industry, which most of our competitors are getting out of as quickly as they can, yet you say you're going to turn around the business…?'" As David said this, he looked as though his courage was sapping away again—could he really convince them?

"Okay David, so that's your next complication." Edwards took another red card, again titled it 'Complication,' and then wrote, reading aloud, "'You are probably wondering how we are going to turn the business around when everyone is saying our market is in decline.' And now we need the Resolution…;" another green card, titled Resolution, "…and I'm guessing the Resolution here will be the customer research you already mentioned…"

"… and the Example will be the Arjun story," said David, reaching for a blue card.

"I think you have the idea. OK, you try the next round. If you paused at this point, what do you think their most likely objection would be?" The professor leaned back in his chair, pleased with the quick progress his new student was making.

"I think they would say, 'What about your competitors? Haven't they figured this out?' I think my answer—my Resolution—is even though the new demand is going to drive prices back up, high enough that we can be quite profitable, for many of our competitors, especially the smaller ones, the prices won't be high enough for them to be viable longer term. One of our competitors has already sold the land their plant is on."

"Very good."

"But I have a question. What if they don't bring up these objections, in this order?"

"You aren't going to wait for them to bring them up, David. You're going to pre-empt them: you're going to bring each complication up yourself. But you can be sure once you do so, they're going to be thinking 'that's exactly what I was wondering!' The role of the complication is to keep *raising an important question in their mind*, which you then answer for them. In fact, you're not going to give them *any* information without first raising a question which that information will answer. Do you see how, if you do this, they will never be bored..."

"Hmmm..." David didn't sound *quite* convinced yet.

"The human being is a problem-solving animal. When we become aware of an important problem or question, we feel the *need* to answer it. The S.Co.R.E. method takes advantage of that. You raise a question, which becomes a question in the minds of your audience members—a problem, which they now need to solve—and so the information you give them next, which solves the problem, is very welcome to them. Then you raise another question—and so on. That's how the S.Co.R.E. method works."

"I *think* I am starting to understand. But I want to work on it a bit more."

"Yes, that's what I'd like to propose. Why don't you take some of these cards with you, and keep working on the story. We can meet again tomorrow afternoon and look over it. When you're done, work through this checklist—" Edwards handed him a piece of paper.

"If you can answer 'yes' to each item, then your storyline is ready—which means we can start putting the slides together." [1]

"That's good, because I don't have much time before this board meeting!" David thanked the professor, put his slides and the index cards into his briefcase, and walked out into the already dark night.

---

[1] For information on downloading a copy of the S.Co.R.E. checklist, see the Resources section at the end of this book"

Chapter Eight

Choosing a Good Chart

DAVID WALKED UP THE STAIRS to Professor Edwards' office. He had spent a couple of hours on the storyline. He thought it was a good storyline, but he was still a little unsure of where this was going. He had 41 index cards—that's fewer than his 75 slides, but was it enough of an improvement?

Professor Edwards was reading at his desk; an old book, with a faded blue cloth cover.

"*Prisoner of Zenda*?" David asked, with a smile.

"No, *Teutonic Knights*, by Henrik Sienkiewicz, the Polish novelist—he won the Nobel prize for literature in 1905."

"Do you spend a lot of time reading fiction?"

"I do." Pleasure seemed to shine outward from inside the professor. "I could tell you I read great stories because, as a professor of communication, I learn a lot about storytelling this way. I do learn a lot; but that's not the main reason I read great fiction. I read because of the immense joy it gives me. I have met some of the greatest characters who have ever lived—on earth or in the minds of their authors—and I feel as if they're my friends, I know them that well. But that's not why you came here. How's your storyline?"

"Pretty good, I think." David sat down, drew a pile of index cards out of his briefcase, and led the professor though them. The whole process took about three minutes.

Edwards complimented him. "This is good; it works. So you're now ready to move on to the graphical stage of designing your presentation. The first thing we want to do is figure out which charts to use. You have a lot of tables, and some charts. Ideally, wherever you have a table, if at all possible you should replace it with a chart, because visuals communicate better than numbers: numbers can *suggest* relationships, differences, patterns, but visuals *demonstrate* them. The charts you do have—everything seems to be either a pie chart or a bar chart. Nothing wrong with those, but there are many more different types of charts, so let's just be sure you're using a good one each time. You might find this helpful."

Edwards gave David a one-page diagram with a variety of different charts all around the perimeter. In the center of the diagram, it had the words "What would you like to show?" and then from those words, several lines moved out in different directions, branching toward the different charts.

"This is the 'Chart Chooser,'" he said. "The way to use this, is you ask yourself, 'What am I trying to show with this chart?'

Figure 3: The Chart Chooser

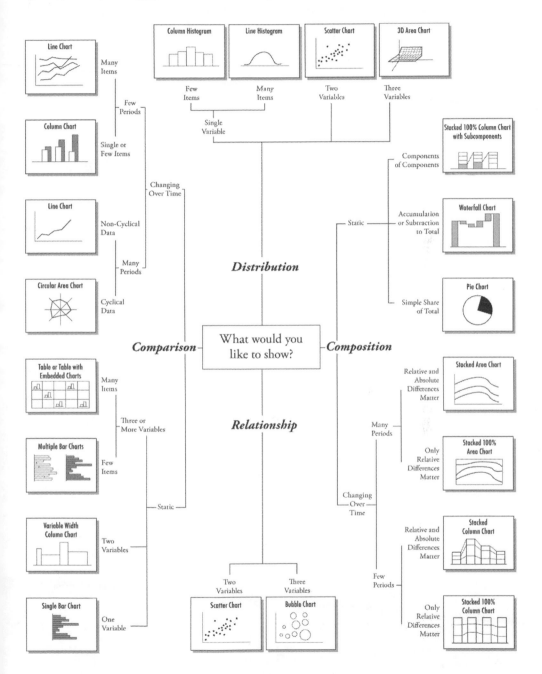

You then follow the lines, answering the subsequent questions along the way, and it'll suggest a chart type you could use. Try it out—go through each of your S.Co.R.E. cards, and for each one that represents any quantitative data, use the Chart Chooser to pick a good chart."

Professor Edwards picked up his copy of *Teutonic Knights*, and sat back while David started flipping through his index cards. In a few minutes, David said, "I think I'm done. But I have a question. I have 41 cards—if each one of these is a slide, then I'll have 41 slides, which is less than my 75, but that's still too many, isn't it?"

Chapter Nine

Grouping Your Slides

"YES, IT IS. But you're assuming a 1-1 mapping between your index cards and slides. Don't do that. What we *want* to do is to try to get as many cards on each slide as possible—because that will mean fewer slides, and fewer slides is almost always better when using Conference room style."

"Why better?"

"Well, David, has anyone ever said to you: 'that was a great presentation, only—you could have used a few more slides'?"

"*Touché.* No, they haven't."

"The main reasons for having fewer slides are two. The first reason comes from research: we know when you show more steps in your logic on one slide, people understand you more easily, and are more likely to be persuaded. Fewer slides mean more steps in your logic on each slide. If you had a seven-step process that you wanted to explain, for example, the research suggests it will make more sense for your audience if you show all of the steps on one slide, rather than breaking it down into three or four, or seven, slides."

David interrupted: "But doesn't that make for really messy, crowded slides?"

"Not necessarily—it's all in how you design them. I'll show you what I mean in a minute. The second reason for having fewer slides is a practical one: the fewer slides you have, the more effort you can spend on each to make it just right. If you only had 10 to 15 slides, you could afford to do a much better job on each than on your 75, right?"

"10 to 15! You mean I have to cut my 75 slides down to 10 or 15? I don't think I can do that."

"Before I tell you whether I think you can or not, David, let me ask *you* a question: what do you think is the theoretical, ideal number of slides in a Conference room style presentation?"

"I don't know—maybe 15, 20?"

"No. The theoretical, ideal number of slides is *one*."

"*One slide?!*"

"Yes, one. Because if you could do the job in one slide, then why would you use two? If you could do it in two, then why would you use three, or five? I'm not saying that you always have to have only one slide, or even that you'll get to one slide often. But if you aim for one, you might get down to five, or seven, but if you aim for 20 you'll get 30 or more."

"I still don't see how I'm going to get all my material onto

10 or 15 slides, let alone seven, or five. Especially if I have to stay at 24 point font or higher, so everyone in the room can read them."

Professor Edwards carefully removed *Teutonic Knights* from his desk, and placed it back on the shelf behind him. "I see, David, that it is now time for us to get back to the topic of the differences between Ballroom and Conference room style presentations. You've read *Presentation Zen* and *Slide:ology*, right?"

"Yes, I have. I think they're excellent."

"They are indeed excellent. If you've read them, you know what a good Ballroom style presentation should look like: minimal text, with attractive, relevant images, and projected slides. They're ideal for when you're trying to inform or entertain a large audience. But when you're trying to persuade a small audience to make a particular decision or take a specific action, then Conference room style is more appropriate.

Professor Edwards continued: "The three important things about conference room style presentations are: they have extensive—but always relevant—detail; they are *printed*, not projected; and every slide must pass the squint test."

"What's the squint test?"

"The squint test is: when you squint at each slide, do you 'get' something about the slide, even if you can't read any of the text? Take a look at this slide."

Edwards grabbed one of David's slides, at random. It contained a series of bullet points. "If you squint at this slide, can you tell me what it's about?"

"Um, no."

"So it doesn't pass the squint test." Edwards then pulled a sheet of paper with a graphic on it from his desk drawer. "How about this; squint at it and tell me if you can guess what it's about. Actually—don't bother squinting—there's no text on it at all, anyway."

The graphic on the sheet of paper looked something like this:

Figure 4: Passing the Squint Test

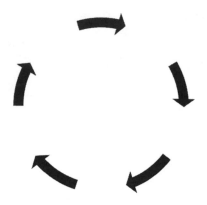

David looked at the paper and said, "It looks like some kind of a cycle."

"Exactly. You didn't read any text, I didn't tell you anything about it, and you figured out, from the very first second you saw it, that it was about some kind of a cycle. There's another example..." Edwards pointed to the map on the wall David had been examining the day before.

"I was going to ask you about that," David said. "What's it about?"

"What do *you* think it's about?"

"It looks like a map, with some kind of flow on it. There's

this orange band flowing one way and then the black one going the other way."

"Exactly. It's a map tracing Napoleon's march on Moscow—that's the orange band, and then his retreat, that's the black one. It was created by Charles Joseph Minard, a Frenchman, and popularized by Edward Tufte. Do you know Tufte's work?"

Figure 5: The Minard Map

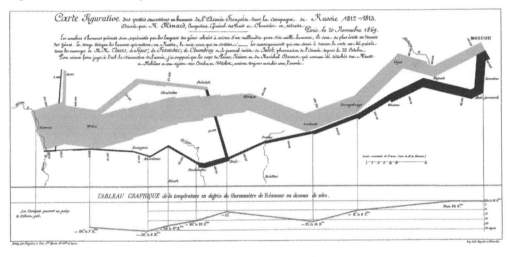

"*That's* where I've seen it before—I knew it looked familiar. I took Tufte's course, but it was years ago."

"Did you like what he said, David?"

"Yes, very inspiring."

"Good, because everything we're talking about here is perfectly consistent with what he teaches. In fact, you can think of the Extreme Presentation method as "applied Tufte," if you like. So, in the map, Minard shows us the number of troops Napoleon took into Russia—that's the thickness of the orange band. And you can see the number of troops shrinking along the way, as men die in battle, or from starvation, or they desert.

"You can see major geographical features, like rivers, you can see the locations of battles, and then the black line shows the dwindling number of troops on retreat. Napoleon led 400,000 troops into this campaign, and came back with only 10,000."

"Wow."

"Yes, do you see how nicely Minard shows all of that on his 'slide'? That's the slide layout, working for you. Slide layout is the most underused, yet one of the most powerful, tools in presentation design. If a slide passes the squint test, then you can put a large amount of detail all over it, and it won't seem too 'busy,' because your audience will immediately understand what the slide is about, and they won't be overwhelmed by the detail."

"But wait a minute," David interrupted. "I thought I read somewhere that if you put lots of text on a slide, and talk at the same time, that's worse than having no slides at all, because your audience tries to listen to you and read at the same time, and ends up doing neither very well."

"That's correct, David, and that's why you never want to have very much text on a *Ballroom style* slide. But with Conference room style, it's different. It's because of the squint test: the theory is that if a slide passes the squint test, the audience doesn't feel a need to read everything on the slide, because they already have some idea of what the slide is about, so they're willing to listen to you as you talk them through the slide."

"I see. Okay, where do we go from here?"

"What you want to do next is take your S.Co.R.E. cards, and

group them according to how many cards you think will fit on each slide. Start at the beginning, take your first card, then your second, and so on, and see how many you think you can fit in one slide. Once you think you have enough, stack those cards.

"Then continue; see how many cards you think you can fit on your next slide, and that's your second stack. And so on, until you've gone through all your cards; the number of stacks you have will be the number of slides you need. Try it now; and remember some of your cards, typically your complications, take up no space at all on a slide, because they are usually just spoken transitions—for example, you might say 'You are wondering how we could be talking about revenue growth when our market is in decline'—but you wouldn't put anything on the slide. Go ahead and try this now, while I go get some coffee."

Chapter Ten

Laying Out Your Slides

PROFESSOR EDWARDS RETURNED A FEW MINUTES LATER with a couple of tall lattes from the Starbucks downstairs.

David had a look on his face that was part self-satisfaction, part astonishment. "I can hardly believe it," he said. "It looks like I only need *four* slides!"

"Now we're talking!" yelled Edwards. "Welcome to the world of Conference room style presentations."

"But aren't the board members going to think this is odd—aren't they going to think I haven't done my homework, if I show up with only four slides?"

"Quite the contrary, David. What I have seen, time and time again, is that while you as the *presenter* might think you have too few slides, the *audience's* reaction is entirely the opposite:

when you show up with a small number of very well designed slides—because of course if you only have four slides you have time to do each one right—they think 'wow—this guy must really understand the issue if he's able to boil it down so succinctly for us.' Of course, you can always have lots of backup slides as well."

"Well, I'm willing to give it a try. So now, I have to come up with some design that passes the squint test, for each of my slides? That could take a while; I was never very good at drawing."

"Actually, there are a bunch of things that can save you a lot of time here, David. The first thing is, if you go to the Extreme Presentation website, you can find 36 different layouts that pass the squint test; feel free to use any of those."[2]

"Second thing: is your office using PowerPoint 2007 or 2010?"

"I think we're on 2007. Why?"

"It has this feature called SmartArt, which is really helpful. SmartArt makes it really easy to create layouts that pass the squint test, and to modify them very easily; all the fonts change size automatically, and all the pieces of the graphic adjust automatically. It's very good. Look at this."

Professor Edwards turned his monitor so David could see; a blank PowerPoint slide was open on the screen. Edwards then showed him how to use the SmartArt feature in PowerPoint.

"See David—look at these buttons—you have all these options: lists, processes, cycles, hierarchies, relationships, and so

---

[2] For information on downloading the 36 layouts, see the Resources section at the end of this book

on. If I click on relationships, here are a bunch of layouts representing relationships. Let's say I want to create a slide to make a point about two ideas in tension. I could pick this one, "Counterbalance Arrows."

A graphic appeared on the slide, looking something like this:

Figure 6: Smart Art

"I can add in text, change the size of the thing, and so on. SmartArt will keep everything in proportion. Try it out when you get back to your office."

"I will."

"And finally, the third thing—check out www.Powerframeworks.com. This is a website with *thousands* of slide layouts, all created by professional designers, and most of these pass the squint test as well. It's not free—I think it's something like $250/year, but totally worth it. Basically, all you have to do is find the layouts you need, download them and fill in the details. Sound good?"

David nodded in agreement.

"Okay, why don't you work on your four slides. We'll meet again tomorrow afternoon and we can do a dry run. Your board meeting is the day after that, isn't it?"

"Yes, it is. Do you mind if I bring Barbara, my boss, to our rehearsal tomorrow?"

"Has she been working with you on this presentation?"

"No, she herself admitted she'd be no help—she's notorious for her own 'Death by PowerPoint' decks."

"By all means, bring her; it'll be interesting to see her reaction."

Chapter Eleven

The Dress Rehersal

"BARBARA WILL BE HERE IN A FEW MINUTES, Professor." David handed him a four-page, black-and-white slide deck. "Before she arrives, could you look over my slides and see how I'm doing on the squint test?"

"Sure David—let's see what you have."

Edwards flipped through the slides. Pausing on the second slide, he said, "As I squint at this, it looks like you have something pushing downward on the left, and then something pushing upward on the right."

Figure 7: Squinting at Slide Two

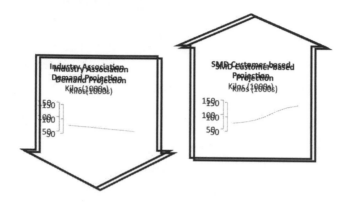

"Kind of. The left arrow shows our industry association forecasts, which predict a continued decline in demand, and the right arrow shows the results of our own survey, which actually show *increased* demand. So do you think this one passes the squint test?"

"I think so—yes, it does. Let me see the next one... I see a column chart—but all the columns are touching each other—is it an area chart—no, wait, I see it, it's a cost curve, right? The cost curve for your industry?"

"Exactly! This is the slide where I show what's going to happen to our competitors as a result of the pricing change. I actually had a question about this one, though, whether it really passes the squint test. I found it on PowerFrameworks.com, which you recommended to me. But it's a chart, not a layout, so does it pass the squint test?"

"That's not a problem, David. If you have a chart that's detailed enough that it's worth filling the whole slide with, then it will automatically pass the squint test, because people will recognize it for what it is—a pie chart, a line graph, a cost curve—as I just did right now, without having to read any of the text. Which, by definition, means it passes the squint test."

There was a knock at the door, and Barbara walked in. David introduced her to Professor Edwards, and handed her a copy of the presentation. After greeting the professor, she flipped through the slides. She looked uncomfortable.

"Professor Edwards, earlier today David was telling me about this Conference room style approach you've been teaching him, but I confess I'm not sure I'm getting it. His presentation is tomorrow, and all we have here are four black-and-white, very crowded slides, which he's telling me he's not even planning to project on a screen. They seem so—well—boring! To be honest, I'm a little worried right now."

"Barbara, I understand your concern. You're falling into a common trap many presenters fall into, wanting your presentation to look eye-catching. The thing is, though, you can't *add* interest to a presentation by putting in fancy graphics, color, transitions, or—heaven forbid—*clipart*. In fact, a lot of research shows that in our kind of presentation, where you're trying to persuade the audience to make a specific decision, those kinds of additions actually work *against* you, because they distract your audience.

"What you need to do, instead of attempting to add interest, is to draw out the inherent interest in your material, by making sure it's *solving a problem for your audience*. This is what David is doing here—and very well, actually.

"I know this approach is new to you, Barbara, and it's feeling risky because you have this critical presentation to the board tomorrow. Let me give you two good reasons why you can have confidence in this method.

"First, Conference room style is founded on extensive empirical research about persuasion. The research shows if you're trying to persuade people to make a particular decision, or take a specific action, you need three things: you need to give them the necessary details, you need interactive discussion, and you need to avoid any distractions. Conference room style presentations do this better than any other style. Because they have lots of detail on them; because they're on paper handouts instead of projected on the screen, and so they enable much more open and interactive discussion; and because they're free of clipart, or transitions, or any other kind of distraction.

"The second reason is, this style of presentation has been pilot tested, and is being used, in several leading companies: companies like ExxonMobil, Kimberly-Clark, eBay, Motorola, HJ Heinz, WW Grainger, Burger King…. It's even used at Microsoft, the makers of PowerPoint themselves.

"Let's try this. We'll have David go through his rehearsal, and you can put yourself in the position of the board members. See if it makes sense to you."

Barbara sat down, still looking uncomfortable. David began his presentation. He talked through the four slides, explaining the details on each one. Playing her role as board member, Barbara asked tough questions about anticipated growth in the cell phone market and implications for raw materials demand, about the customer data, and about implementation timing, all of which David handled well. At the end of the discussion, Barbara's tone had changed completely. She sat back, smiled, and said, "Well, I think you have something here. I have to admit—I wasn't very comfortable before, but I think this could just work!"

Chapter Twelve

The Presentation

IT DOESN'T MATTER HOW MANY PRESENTATIONS you have given in your life—when the stakes are high, most people still experience stage fright. It's always at its worst in the moments just before the presentation begins. Which is why David was sitting outside the boardroom, with his heart beating well above its normal rate, waiting for his turn.

He looked over his presentation once again. The professor had suggested that—since he was using a Conference room style presentation, where slides are printed, not projected—he should write his notes for each slide on the back of the preceding slide. This way while his audience were looking down at their own copies of the slide deck, he could refer to his notes and they wouldn't even notice.

A moment later, the secretary of the board opened the door and invited him to enter. David strode in, with copies of his presentation in his hands, and passed them around the boardroom table. The chairman invited David to begin, and so he did.

Good afternoon. Thank you for allowing me the time to talk to you about the future of the Specialized Materials Division. As we all know, overall corporate profitability for Asprit Industries has been declining. I would like to share with you today a plan to turn around our division, which will add $25 million to the bottom line next year. I am going to be working off the handout I've just passed around...

Slide 1:

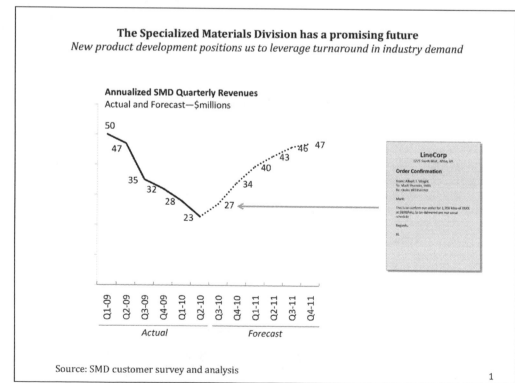

The Specialized Materials Division has a promising future
New product development positions us to leverage turnaround in industry demand

Source: SMD customer survey and analysis

If you look at the first slide, you'll see a chart of our division's quarterly historical revenues on the left side—you are all familiar with the downward trend. But the future looks a lot better. This is our forecast for the next several quarters—it's based on some key new products we've developed, and it shows a much more positive picture."

This is real, not just some naïve 'hockey-stick' projection. To the right of the page I have put a copy of an order we just received from LineCorp, a major customer for our firm, for $1.2 million. I think this order is a vote of confidence in our new approach.

You may be wondering if this order is a fluke. Everything you've heard so far about our market is that it's in permanent decline, so how come I'm giving you these growth predictions right now?

Take a look at the next page, ...

Slide 2:

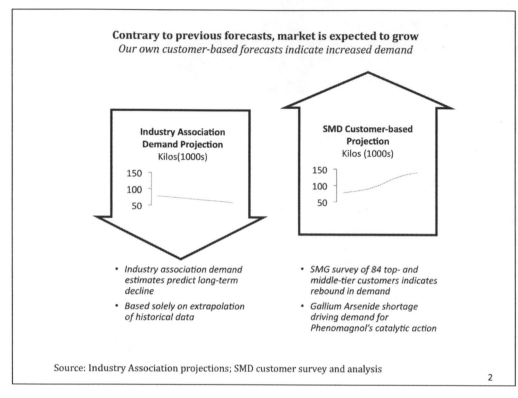

On this page, we're comparing the industry association projections, on the left, with our own survey-based forecast, on the right.

The industry association projections are for continued decline—that's why we've put them in the downward-pointing arrow on the left, and inside the arrow, the actual projections, showing continued decline. The problem we have with these projections is, the association developed them just by extrapolating historical data. They don't say this in their publications, but when we challenged them, they admitted that is how they do it.

So on the right, we have our own forecast. Since we were uncomfortable with the reliability of the association forecast, in order to get a better idea of where this market is heading, we surveyed all of our major customers and most of our mid-sized customers, to understand their supply needs for the upcoming several quarters.

We were surprised, first, how many of our customers answered the survey—there seemed to be a level of interest in our products, among our larger customers, that we had not seen in a while. Even more surprising, though, were their actual responses. Their estimated volumes were much higher than anything we were expecting. You can see this from the upward-pointing arrow, and inside it, our actual forecast.

We wanted to understand this better, so we met in person with each of our largest clients. Let me tell you about one of them, Arjun Kohli—he's the purchasing manager of Spengler, our largest customer. He told us an interesting story. They've been having trouble sourcing one of their key raw materials, Gallium Arsenide, due to a worldwide shortage. Gallium Arsenide is a critical component in cell phone manufacture, and the demand for cell phones and particularly smart phones has strained supply for the material, so they are substituting another, which requires one of our new products, Phenomagnol as a catalyst. Phenomagnol, as you know, is a refined form of our core product.

And we heard this same story again and again—because of the continued shortage of Gallium Arsenide, they are all reformulating and planning to place substantial orders of Phenomagnol, and some of our other new reformulations, from us. That's why we're now confident in forecasting growth.

You may be wondering: what about our competitors? Haven't they figured this out, yet? Please turn to slide three, on the next page...

Slide 3:

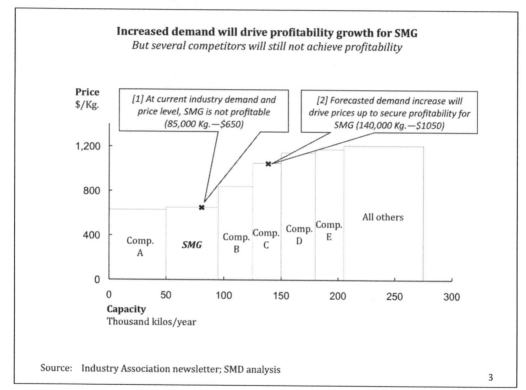

To answer that, we need to look at the cost curve for our industry, which is on this page. The different columns represent the main competitors in our industry—the height of each column is their production cost per ton, and the width is their total annual production capacity.[3]

---

[3] The cost curve chart on which this slide is based is from www.PowerFrameWorks.com.

Box [1] points to the current price. At this price, you can see that our division and Competitor A are barely profitable, and the rest of the industry are losing money. We expect the increased demand to drive price up to $1050 per kilo—that's where Box [2] is pointing—and this makes us profitable. It also makes Competitors A and B profitable, with Competitor C breaking even. But that's likely as high as the price is going to go for the foreseeable future, so Competitors D, E and all of the smaller players, which I labeled here as 'All Others,' are still losing money. So, they're likely going to go ahead with their plans to exit the business, because their costs are just too high to be competitive in the foreseeable future.

Competitor E, for example, has already sold the land its plant is on, and several of the smaller players are converting to other product lines.

It looks like we're going to be in good shape. But there's a cost to this. In order to fulfill this demand at the competitive cost levels on this chart, we need to expand our ability to refine Phenomagnol. And that's why I've asked you for your time today. Turn to the last page ...

Slide 4:

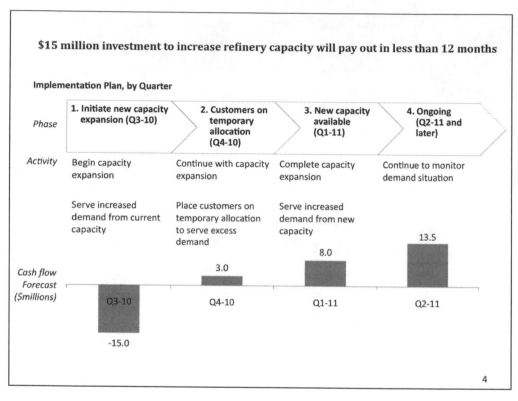

We need $15 million in new capital expenditure next quarter in order to expand our refining ability. On this page, I've laid out our implementation plan, across four quarters. The good news is, we expect the $15 million to pay out within those four quarters.

The chevrons at the top of the page show the four steps, each lasting one fiscal quarter. We'll start with step 1, next quarter, where we begin the capacity expansion, while serving the increased demand for Phenomagnol from our current capacity, which will max out that capacity.

Below that, you can see our cash flow position for that quarter. We barely break even on our operating costs, so we show a net negative cash flow of $15 million, which is the capital expenditure.

The following quarter, Q4, we continue with the capacity expansion, and we'll have to put our customers on allocation, rationing out the Phenomagnol because the new capacity won't be on line yet.

But this situation goes away in the next quarter, and by the fourth quarter, Q2 of next year, the positive cash flow has more than paid back the $15 million. So it's an attractive opportunity, but we need your approval to spend the $15 million today.

David paused. There was a moment of silence. David realized, in that moment, he had gone through his entire presentation, and no one had interrupted him. That was a first.

The moment of silence didn't last long, of course. The questions came, rapid-fire, from several of the board members. They wanted to know more about the survey, about how exactly the $15 million would be spent, why $15 million, and why did we need it all right now. David had answers to all these questions.

What was interesting, though, was that at a certain point, they stopped asking him questions, and started to debate among themselves the merits of David's proposal. Professor Edwards had predicted this would happen. "And when it does," he said, "let them go! It's a sign that they are internalizing your material, and—very likely—they are going to agree with your recommendation."

A few minutes later, the Chairman of the Board turned to David and said, "You and your team have a very solid case here… these are tough times to be asking for investment money … but given the strength of your case, we are going to approve your request for the $15 million. Good work, David!"

SHORTLY AFTERWARD, BARBARA, DAVID, AND THE PROFESSOR were relaxing in Barbara's office, relishing their victory. "My hat's off to you, professor; I confess I never really lost my skepticism about this method until David began speaking. It was amazing none of them interrupted him—that's never happened before."

"I know what you mean, Barbara. There is this belief—I think it's not just with presentations, but with communication in our society in general—that somehow style can make up for content. Perhaps it's because of the prevalence of media, and especially video. The impression seems to be, if I can just make my communication glitzy enough, or catchy enough, people will buy what I'm selling. We can debate to what extent that's true, but one thing's sure: most managers, clients, prospects, and certainly board members, can see right through the fluff. If you want people to act on your ideas these days, you need to strip away all the pizzazz and focus honestly on the details of your idea, and how it helps them solve a problem of theirs."

"And tell a good story!" replied David.

RESOURCES

To learn more about the Extreme Presentation™ method, and

- for free tools and templates
- for copies of Advanced Presentations by Design: Creating Communication that Drives Action, by Dr. Andrew Abela, a complete guide to the Extreme Presentation method and its extensive scientific foundations
- and for the Extreme Presentation blog, featuring the latest ideas on presentation design using the Extreme Presentation method

go to www.ExtremePresentation.com/books/pres

BIBLIOGRAPHY

ABELA, ANDREW V. (2008), Advanced Presentations by Design: Creating Communication that Drives Action (San Francisco, CA: Pfeiffer)

DUARTE, NANCY (2008), Slide:ology: The Art and Science of Creating Great Presentations (Sebastopol, CA: O'Reilly Media)

REYNOLDS, GARR (2008), Presentation Zen: Simple Ideas on Presentation Design and Delivery (Berkeley, CA: New Riders Press)

TUFTE, EDWARD R. (2001), The Visual Display of Quantitative Information. Cheshire, CT: Graphics Press.

ZELAZNY, GENE, (2001) Say it With Charts: The Executive's Guide to Visual Communication (New York, NY: McGraw Hill)

——, (2006), Say It With Presentations: How to Design and Deliver Successful Business Presentations (New York, NY: McGraw Hill)

ACKNOWLEDGEMENTS

I WOULD LIKE TO THANK Edward Abela, Kathleen Abela, Stacey Cox, Paul Radich, Clodagh Reeves, Cathy Rinzma, Stew McHie, Laura Syron, Kathy Villella, Stephanie Zammit, and Gene Zelazny for their very helpful comments on earlier drafts of the book. I would also like to thank the many participants who have attended my Extreme Presentation™ workshops over the years, whose interest and feedback contributed to this book.

ABOUT THE AUTHOR

DR. ANDREW ABELA has been designing and delivering effective presentations to senior executives—and training and coaching others to do so—for over 20 years. He is the Chairman of the Department of Business & Economics at the Catholic University of America in Washington, DC and associate professor of marketing. Prior to this he worked as a brand manager with Procter & Gamble, as a management consultant with McKinsey & Company, and he was the founding managing director of the Marketing Leadership Council, a best-practices research organization serving Chief Marketing Officers at hundreds of leading corporations worldwide. He is also the author of *Advanced Presentations by Design* (Wiley, 2008), which provides a comprehensive review of the extensive empirical research on effective presentation.